Learn to Read Persian

THE TALE OF LITTLE MR. MOUSE AND HIS TAIL

Iranian Folktales for Children

Learn to Read Persian

THE TALE OF LITTLE MR. MOUSE AND HIS TAIL
Iranian Folktales for Children

Persian//English/Vocabulary Lists

Second Edition

Translated by

Shohreh Emami

Assisted by

Jenny Take

Illustrated by

Hossein Faridi

ISBN: 978-1-988385-25-9

Preface

Little Mr. Mouse Books publishes **Learn to Read Persian** folktales based on popular Iranian Folktales. *Learn to Read Persian: The Tale f Little Mr. Mouse and His Tail: Iranian Folktales for Children* is based on the original version of the popular Iranian folktale *The Tale of Little Mr. Mouse and His Tail.*

This learn to read Persian version of *The Tale of Little Mr. Mouse and His Tail* features Persian, Finglish, and English text, along with Persian/Finglish/Enlish vocabulary lists. The Persian and Finglish text are all linked with the vocabulary lists. A vocabulary list which shows the shapes of the Persian letters according to their place in a word is also included.

The poetic, rhythmic nature of *The Tale of Little Mr. Mouse and His Tail* helps with vocabulary retention. It is an enjoyable read.

learnreadpersianstories.com

Once upon a time......

یکی[1] بود[2] یکی نبود[3]، زیر[4]-ه گنبد[5] کبود[6]، غیر از[7] خدا[8] هیچکس نبود[9].

Yeki[1] bood[2] yeki nabood[3], zir[4]-e gonbad-e[5] kabood[6], gheir az[7] Khodaa[8] hichkas nabood[9].

1	یکی	yeki	someone
2	بود	bood	was
3	نبود	nabood	was not
4	زیر	zir	under
5	گنبد	gonbad	dome
6	کبود	kabood	blue
7	غیراز	gheir az	other than
8	خدا	Khodaa	God
9	هیچکس نبود	hichkas nabood	There was no one

There was a Mr. Mouse whose tail got cut off when he went into a hole.

یک آقا موشه[1] ای بود که[2] رفت[3] تو[4] سوراخ[5] دمش[6] پاره[7] شد.

Yek Aaqaa Moosheh[1]-ee bood keh[2] raft[3] too[4] sooraakh[5] domesh[6] paareh shod[7].

1	آقا موشه	Aaqaa Moosheh	Mr. Mouse
2	که	keh	that (whose)
3	رفت	raft	went
4	تو	too	in
5	سوراخ	sooraakh	a hole
6	دمش	domesh	his tail
7	پاره شد	paareh shod	got cut

He went to the Cobbler and said, "Cobbler, please sew my tail back on. Tomorrow is Norooz, and everyone has a tail except me."

رفت پیش[1] پینه دوز[2] و[3] گفت[4]: «پینه دوز دممو[5] بدوز[6]. فردا[7] که عید نوروزه[8]. همه[9] دم[10] دارن[11] من[12] ندارم[13].»

Raft pish[1]-e Pineh dooz[2] o[3] goft[4]: "Pineh dooz domamo[5] be-dooz[6]. Fardaa[7] keh Aid-e Norooz-e[8] hameh[9] dom[10] daaran[11] man[12] nadaaram[13]."

1	رفت پیش	raft pish-e	went to
2	پینه دوز	Pineh dooz	Cobbler
3	و	o (va written)	and
4	گفت	goft	said
5	دممو	domamo	my tail
6	بدوز	bedooz	sew
7	فردا	fardaa	tomorrow
8	عید نوروزه	Aid-e Norooz-e	New Year's holiday
9	همه	hameh	all
10	دم	dom	tail
11	دارن	daaran	They have
12	من	man	I
13	ندارم	nadaaram	I do not have

The Cobbler said, "Go and get some thread from the Spinner and bring it to me. Then, I will sew your tail back on."

پینه دوز گفت:«برو`برا`من از`جولا`نخ`بگیر`تا`من دمتو`بدوزم`.»

Pineh dooz goft: "boro[1] baraa[2] man az[3] Joolaa[4] nakh[5] begir[6] taa[7] man dometo[8] bedoozam[9]."

1	برو	boro	go
2	برا	baraa	for
3	از	az	from
4	جولا	Joolaa	Spinner
5	نخ	nakh	thread
6	بگیر	begir	get and bring
7	تا	taa	then
8	دمتو	dometo	your tail
9	بدوزم	bedoozam	I sew

Mr. Mouse went to the Spinner and said," Spinner, please give me some thread for the Cobbler so he can sew my tail back on. Tomorrow is Norooz, and everyone has a tail except me."

آقا موشه رفت پیش جولا و گفت: «جولا نخو ده[1]، نخو پینه دوز دممو بدوز. فردا که عید نوروزه همه دم دارن من ندارم ».

Aaqaa Moosheh raft pish-e Joolaa o goft: "Joolaa nakho deh[1], nakho Pineh dooz domamo bedooz. Fardaa keh Aid-e Norooz-e hameh dom daaran man nadaaram."

1	ده	deh	You give

The Spinner said, "Go and get an egg from the Chicken and bring it to me. Then, I will give you some thread."

جولا گفت: «برو از جوجو١ برا من تخم٢ بگیر تا من بهت٣ نخ بدم۴.»

Joolaa goft: "boro az Joojoo[1] baraa man tokhm[2] begir taa man behet[5] nakh bedam[4]."

1	جوجو	Joojoo	Chicken
2	تخم	tokhm	egg
3	بهت	behet	to you
4	بدم	bedam	I give

Mr. Mouse went to the Chicken and said, "Chicken, please give me an egg. I will give the egg to the Spinner; the Spinner will give me some thread. I will give the thread to the Cobbler; the Cobbler will then sew on my tail. Tomorrow is Norooz, and everyone has a tail except me."

آقا موشه رفت پیش جوجو و گفت: «جوجو تخمو ده، تخمو جولا دم`1`، جولا نخو ده، نخو پینه دوز دممو بدوز. فردا که عید نوروزه همه دم دارن من ندارم.»

Aaqaa Moosheh raft pish-e Joojoo o goft: "Joojoo tokhmo deh, tokhmo Joolaa dam[1], Joolaa nakho deh, nakho Pineh dooz do-mamo bedooz. Fardaa keh Aid-e Norooz-e hameh dom daaran man nadaaram."

1	دم	dam	I give

The Chicken said, "Go and get some millet from the Forage-seller and bring it to me. Then, I will give you an egg."

جوجو گفت: «تو١ برو از علاف٢ برا من ارزن٣ بگیر و بیار٤ تا من بهت تخم بدم.»

Joojoo goft: "toe[1] boro az Allaaf[2] baraa man arzan[3] begir o biaar[4] taa man behet tokhm bedam."

1	تو	toe	you
2	علاف	Allaaf	Forage-seller
3	ارزن	arzan	millet
4	بیار	biaar	bring

Mr. Mouse went to the Forage-seller and said, "Forage-seller, please give me some millet; I will give the millet to the Chicken; the Chicken will give me an egg. I will give the egg to the Spinner; the Spinner will give me some thread. I will give the thread to the Cobbler; the Cobbler will then sew my tail back on. Tomorrow is Norooz, and everyone has a tail except me."

آقا موشه رفت پیش علاف و گفت: «علاف ارزن ده، ارزن جوجو دم، جوجو تخمو ده، تخمو جولا دم، جولا نخو ده، نخو پینه دوز دممو بدوز. فردا که عید نوروزه همه دم دارن من ندارم.»

Aaqaa Moosheh raft pish-e Allaaf o goft: "Allaaf arzan deh, arzan Joojoo dam, Joojoo tokhmo deh, tokhmo Joolaa dam, Joolaa nakho deh, nakho Pineh dooz domamo bedooz. Fardaa keh Aid-e Norooz-e hameh dom daaran man nadaaram."

The Forage-seller said, "Go and get a large sieve from the Gypsy and bring it to me. Then, I will give you some millet."

Mr. Mouse went to the Gypsy and said, "Gypsy, please give me a large sieve. I will give the large sieve to the Forage-seller; the Forage-seller will give me some millet. I will give the millet to the Chicken; the Chicken will give me an egg. I will give the egg to the Spinner; the Spinner will give me some thread. I will give the thread to the Cobbler; the Cobbler will then sew my tail back on. Tomorrow is Norooz, and everyone has a tail except me."

علاف گفت: «برو از کولی ۱ برا من غربال ۲ بگیر تا من بهت ارزن بدم.» آقا موشه رفت پیش کولی و گفت: «کولی غربال ده، غربال علاف دم، علاف ارزن ده، ارزن جوجو دم، جوجو تخمو ده، تخمو جولا دم، جولا نخو ده، نخو پینه دوز دممو بدوز. فردا که عید نوروزه همه دم دارن من ندارم.»

Allaaf goft: "boro az Koli[1] baraa man gharbaal[2] begir taa man behet arzan bedam." Aaqaa Moosheh raft pish-e Koli o goft: "Koli gharbaal deh, gharbaal Allaaf dam, Allaaf arzan deh, arzan Joojoo dam, Joojoo tokhmo deh, tokhmo Joolaa dam, Joolaa nakho deh, nakho Pineh dooz domamo bedooz. Fardaa keh Aid-e Norooz-e hameh dom daaran man nadaaram."

1	کولی	Koli	Gypsy
2	غربال	gharbaal	large sieve

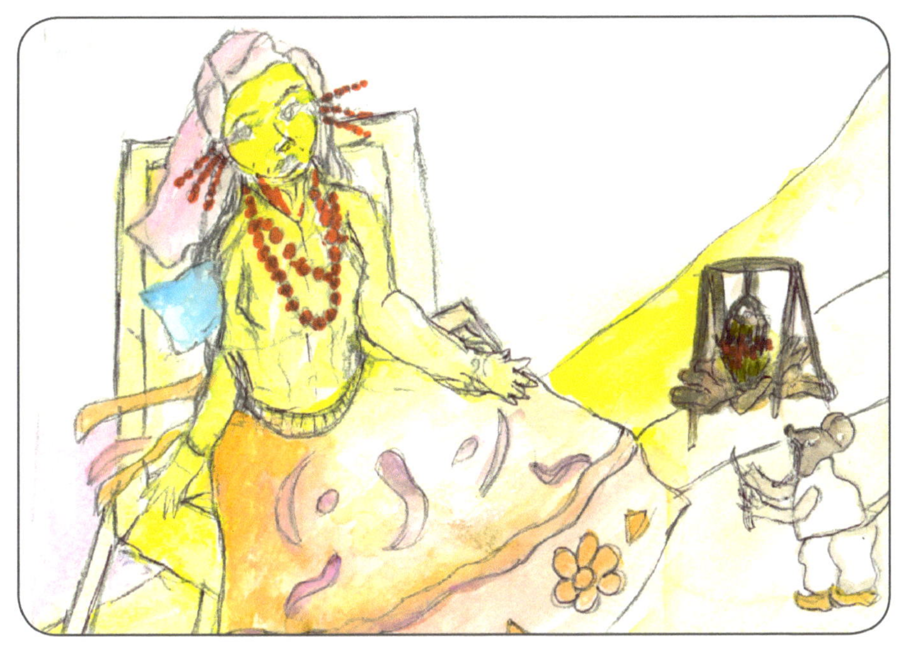

The Gypsy said, "Go and get some stiff cord from the Goat and bring it to me. Then I will give you a large sieve." Mr. Mouse went to the Goat and said, "Goat, please give me some stiff cord. I will give the stiff cord to the Gypsy; the Gypsy will give me a large sieve. I will give the large sieve to the Forage-seller; the Forage-seller will give me some millet. I will give the millet to the Chicken; the Chicken will give me an egg. I will give the egg to the Spinner; the Spinner will give me some thread. I will give the thread to the Cobbler; the Cobbler will then sew my tail back on. Tomorrow is Norooz, and everyone has a tail except me."

کولی گفت: «برو از بزی[1] برا من روده[2] بگیر و بیار تا من بهت غربال بدم.» آقا موشه رفت پیش بزی و گفت: «بزی روده ده، روده کولی دم، کولی غربال ده، غربال علاف دم، علاف ارزن ده، ارزن جوجو دم، جوجو تخمو ده، تخمو جولا دم، جولا نخو ده، نخو پینه دوز دممو بدوز. فردا که عید نوروزه همه دم دارن من ندارم.»

Koli goft: "boro az Bozi[1] baraa man roodeh[2] begir o biaar taa man behet gharbaal bedam." Aaqaa Moosheh raft pish-e Bozi o goft: "Bozi roodeh deh, roodeh Koli dam, Koli gharbaal deh, gharbaal Allaaf dam, Allaaf arzan deh, Arzan Joojoo dam, Joo-joo tokhmo deh, tokhmo Joolaa dam, Joolaa nakho deh, nak-ho Pineh dooz domamo bedooz. Fardaa keh Aid-e Norooz-e hameh dom daaran man nadaaram."

1	بز	Boz	Goat
2	روده	roodeh	Intestine/Stiff cord

The Goat said, "Go and get some grass from the Earth and bring it to me. Then I will give you some stiff cord." Mr. Mouse went to the Earth and said, "Earth, Please give me some grass. I will give the grass to the Goat; the Goat will give me some stiff cord. I will give the stiff cord to the Gypsy; the Gypsy will give me a large sieve. I will give the large sieve to the Forage-seller; the Forage-seller will give me some millet. I will give the millet to the Chicken; the Chicken will give me an egg. I will give the egg to the Spinner; the Spinner will give me some thread. I will give the thread to the Cobbler; the Cobbler will then sew my tail back on. Tomorrow is Norooz, and everyone has a tail except me."

بزی گفت: «تو برو از زمین` برا من علف` بگیر تا من بهت روده بدم.» آقا موشه رفت پیش زمین و گفت: «زمین علف ده، علف بزی دم، بزی روده ده، روده کولی دم، کولی غربال ده، غربال علاف دم، علاف ارزن ده، ارزن جوجو دم، جوجو تخمو ده، تخمو جولا دم، جولا نخو ده، نخو پینه دوز دممو بدوز. فردا که عید نوروزه همه دم دارن من ندارم.»

Bozi goft: "toe boro az Zamin[1] baraa man alaf[2] begir taa man behet roodeh bedam." Aaqaa Moosheh raft pish-e Zamin o goft: "Zamin alaf deh, alaf Bozi dam, Bozi roodeh deh, roodeh Koli dam, Koli gharbaal deh, gharbaal Allaaf dam, Allaaf arzan deh, arzan Joojoo dam, Joojoo tokhmo deh, tokhmo Joolaa dam, Joolaa nakho deh, nakho Pineh dooz domamo bedooz. Fardaa keh Aid-e Norooz-e hameh dom daraan man nadaar-am."

1	زمین	Zamin	The Earth/ground
2	علف	alaf	grass

The Earth said, "If you would like some grass, you should go to the Spring and get some water for me. Then, I will give you some grass." Mr. Mouse went to the Spring and said, "Spring, please give me some water. I will give the water to the Earth; the Earth will give me some grass. I will give the grass to the Goat; the Goat will give me some stiff cord. I will give the stiff cord to the Gypsy; the Gypsy will give me a large sieve. I will give the large sieve to the Forage-seller; the Forage-seller will give me some millet. I will give the millet to the Chicken; the Chicken will give me an egg. I will give the egg to the Spinner; the Spinner will give me some thread. I will give the thread to the Cobbler; the Cobbler will then sew my tail back on. Tomorrow is Norooz, and everyone has a tail except me."

زمین گفت: «اگه١ علف میخوای٢ باید٣ از چشمه٤ برا من آب٥ بگیری، تا من بهت علف بدم.» آقا موشه رفت پیش چشمه و گفت: «چشمه آبو ده، آبو زمین دم، زمین علف ده، علف بزی دم، بزی روده ده، روده کولی دم، کولی غربال ده، غربال علاف دم، علاف ارزن ده، ارزن جوجو دم، جوجو تخمو ده، تخمو جولا دم، جولا نخو ده، نخو پینه دوز دممو بدوز. فردا که عید نوروزه همه دم دارن من ندارم.»

Zamin goft: "Ageh[1] alaf mikhaai[2] baayad[3] az Cheshmeh[4] baraa man aab[5] begiri taa man behet alaf bedam." Aaqaa Moosheh raft pish-e Cheshmeh o goft: "Cheshmeh aabo deh, aabo Zamin dam, Zamin alaf deh, alaf Bozi dam, Bozi roodeh deh, roodeh Koli dam, Koli gharbaal deh, gharbaal Allaaf dam, Allaaf arzan deh, arzan Joojoo dam, Joojoo tokhmo deh, tokhmo Joolaa dam, Joolaa nakho deh, nakho Pineh dooz domamo bedooz. Fardaa keh Aide Norooz hameh dom daaran man nadaaram."

1	اگه	ageh	if
2	میخوای	mikhaai	want
3	باید	baayad	should
4	چشمه	Cheshmeh	Spring
5	آب	aab	water

The Spring gave him some water.

He gave the water to the Earth; the Earth gave him some grass.

He gave the grass to the Goat; the Goat gave him some stiff cord.

He gave the stiff cord to the Gypsy; the Gypsy gave him a large sieve.

He gave the large sieve to the Forage-seller; the Forage-seller gave him some millet.

He gave the millet to the Chicken; the Chicken gave him an egg.

He gave the egg to the Spinner; the Spinner gave him some thread.

He gave the thread to the Cobbler, and then the Cobbler sewed his tail back on.

Tomorrow is Norooz, and everyone has a tail, including our Little Mr. Mouse.

چشمه بهش¹ آب داد².

آبو داد به زمین، زمین بهش علف داد.

علفو داد به بزی، بزی بهش روده داد.

روده رو داد به کولی، کولی بهش غربال داد.

غربالو داد به علاف، علاف بهش ارزن داد.

ارزنو داد به جوجو، جوجو بهش تخم داد.

تخمو داد به جولا، جولا بهش نخ داد.

نخو داد به پینه دوز، پینه دوز دمشو دوخت³.

فردا که عید نوروزه همه دم دارن. آقا موشه ما هم⁴ دم داره.

Cheshmeh behesh[1] aab daad[2].

Aabo daad beh Zamin, Zamin behesh alaf daad.

Alafo daad beh Bozi, Bozi behesh roodeh daad.

Roodeh ro daad beh Koli, Koli behesh gharbaal daad.

Gharbaalo daad beh Allaaf, Allaaf behesh arzan daad.

Arzano daad beh Joojoo, Joojoo behesh tokhm daad.

Tokhmo daad beh Joolaa, Joolaa behesh nakh daad.

Nakho daad beh Pineh dooz, Pineh dooz domesho dookht[3].

Fardaa keh Aid-e Norooz-e hameh dom daaran, Aaqaa Moosheh maa ham[4] dom daareh.

1	بهش	behesh	to someone
2	داد	daad	gave
3	دوخت	dookht	sewed
4	هم	ham	also

Our story has come to an end. The crow's trip has not finished yet.
We went up and found our story to be true.
We came down and found our story to be made-up.

قصه ما به سر رسید   کلاغه به خونه اش نرسید

بالا رفتیم ماست بود   قصه ما راست بود

پایین آمدیم دوغ بود   قصه ما دروغ بود

Qeseh maa beh sar resid   *Kalagheh beh khoonash naresid*

Baala raftim maast bood   *Qeseh maa raast bood*

Pain aamadim doogh bood   *Qeseh maa doroogh bood*

Persian Alphabet

	START	MIDDLE	END	PRONOUNCIATION
ا	اَ اُ اِ	ـا	ـا	a,e,o (short)
آ	آ	ـا	ـا	aa (long a)
ب	بـ	ـبـ	ـب	b
پ	پـ	ـپـ	ـپ	p
ت	تـ	ـتـ	ـت	t
ث	ثـ	ـثـ	ـث	s
ج	جـ	ـجـ	ـج	j
چ	چـ	ـچـ	ـچ	ch
ح	حـ	ـحـ	ـح	h
خ	خـ	ـخـ	ـخ	kh
د	د	ـد	ـد	d
ذ	ذ	ـذ	ـذ	z
ر	ر	ـر	ـر	r
ز	ز	ـز	ـز	z
ژ	ژ	ـژ	ـژ	zh
س	سـ	ـسـ	ـس	s
ش	شـ	ـشـ	ـش	sh
ص	صـ	ـصـ	ـص	s

	START	MIDDLE	END	PRONOUNCIATION
ض	ـض	ـضـ	ض	z
ط	ط	ـطـ	ط	t
ظ	ظ	ـظـ	ظ	z
ع	ـع	ـعـ	ع	'
غ	ـغ	ـغـ	غ	gh
ف	ف	ـفـ	ف	f
ق	ق	ـقـ	ق	q
ک	ک	ـکـ	ک	k
گ	گ	ـگـ	گ	g
ل	ل	ـلـ	ل	l
م	مـ	ـمـ	م	m
ن	نـ	ـنـ	ن	n
و	و	و	و	va (written) oo (spoken)
ہ	ھ	ـہـ	ـہ	h
ی	یـ	ـیـ	ی	ee

Request for Book Reviews

Thank you for reading **Learn to Read Persian: The Tale of Little Mr. Mouse and His Tail: Iranian Folktales for Children.** We hope your students found this book to be a fun and easy way to learn how to read Persian.

We would love to hear from you. If you enjoyed this book, please leave an honest review on **Learn to Read Persian: The The Tale of Little Mr. Mouse and His Tail: Iranian Folktales for Children (Book 1)**'s Amazon's detail page.

A review of one or two sentences will be much appreciated.

Thank you,

Jenny Take

Jenny Take
Little Mr. Mouse Books
(littlemrmousebooks@gmail.com)

About the Translator and Illustrator

Shohreh Emami

In 2007, Shohreh Emami immigrated to Canada from Iran.

As a child in Iran, Shohreh Emami enjoyed listening to Persian folktales that had been passed down to her mother. Later, when she told these folktales to her grandchildren, she realized that there was a language barrier. She then rewrote these Iranian folktales in modern-day Persian and then translated them into English. These Iranian folktales are being published by **Little Mr. Mouse Books** as **Learn to Read Persian** folktales. **Little Mr. Mouse Books** also publishes English versions of these Iranian folktales.

Shohreh Emami lives in Halifax, Nova Scotia, Canada.

Hossein Faridi

In 2007, Hossein Faridi immigrated to Canada from Iran.

Hossein Faridi is the illustrator for **Little Mr. Mouse Books**. His handiwork includes the illustrations for the **Learn to Read Persian** folktales. He is also the artist for the English language Persian folktales published by **Little Mr. Mouse Books**.

Hossein Faridi lives in Halifax, Nova Scotia, Canada.

Acknowledgments

Connections Halifax:
Thank you for many years of support and help. *Learn to Read Persian: The Tale of Little Mr. Mouse and His Tail: Iranian Folktales for Children* would not have been possible without you. You are an awesome group of people.

Jenny Take:
Thank you for all you have done to bring *Learn to Read Persian: The Tale of Little Mr. Mouse and His Tail: Iranian Folktales for Children* a reality..

Houra Yavari:
Thank you for your valuable advice and help.

Ramin Nejat:
Thank you for helping me with endless rounds of editing *Learn to Read Persian: The Tale of Little Mr. Mouse and His Tail: Iranian Folktales for Children.*

Shayna Take:
Thank you for your help editing the English text for *Learn to Read Persian: The Tale of Little Mr. Mouse and His Tail: Iranian Folktales for Children.*

Peter Selinger:
Thank you for your meticulous help in editing *Learn to Read Persian: The Tale of Little Mr. Mouse and His Tail: Iranian Folktales for Children.*

Justina Dollard:
Thank you for all your help with the illustration process.

Marzieh Khoshtaghaza (MarzArts):
Thank you for the book cover and interior design. It looks really nice.

Little Mr. Mouse Books

The following books are available on Amazon.

Learn to Read Persian: The Tale of Little Mr. Mouse and His Tail: Iranian Folktales for Children
(Persian, Finglish, English, with Persian/Finglish/English vocabulary lists)

The Rolling Pumpkin: Iranian Folktales for Children

Learn to Read Persian: The Rolling Pumpkin Series

The Rolling Pumpkin: Iranian Folktales for Children. (Book 1)
(Persian, Finglish, English, with Persian/Finglish/English vocabulary lists)

Kadoo-ye qelqeleh zan: Iranian Folktales for Children. (Book 2)
(Persian, with Persian/Finglish/English vocabulary lists)

And there will be more to come……..

learnreadpersianstories.com